ANIMALS OF THE NATIONAL PARKS OF AMERICA

ANIMALS OF THE NATIONAL PARKS OF AMERICA

JAMES MURFIN

GALLERY BOOKS
An Imprint of W. H. Smith Publishers Inc.
112 Madison Avenue
New York City 10016

Endpapers *In Denali National Park and Preserve, a reindeer keeps a watchful eye on the photographer under the towering peak of Mount McKinley, at 20 320 feet the tallest mountain in the United States.*

Half title page *Bison herd at sunset in Badlands National Park, South Dakota.*

Title page *Great egret nesting in a reed bed in the Everglades.*

Contents pages *Brown bears wrestling in McNeil River, Alaska.*

This book was devised and produced by Multimedia Publications (UK) Ltd.

Editor: Marilyn Inglis
Production: Karen Bromley
Design: Terry Allen
Picture Research: Alan Forman, Tessa Paul

First published in the United States of America 1985 by Gallery Books, an imprint of W.H. Smith Publishers Inc., 112 Madison Avenue, New York, NY 10016

ISBN 0 8317 0332 6

Typeset by Keene Graphics
Origination by Scan Studios Ltd., Dublin
Printed in Italy by New Interlitho SpA, Milan

CONTENTS

INTRODUCTION

There are more than 400 species of mammal, nearly 700 species of bird, 300 reptile and 200 amphibian species in North America, and the majority live and are protected in our national parks. The mountains and forests of the parks teem with wildlife of all sorts, sizes, and shapes, from the moose and the bear to the high soaring eagle and the smallest mouse and lizard. Some can be easily seen, while others remain hidden and rarely reveal themselves. The chances of spotting a white-tailed deer, for example, are good, but photographing a grizzly bear or a coyote or bobcat can be most difficult even when something is known of the animal's habits.

Observing wildlife in national parks is one of the great joys in visiting places like Grand Canyon, Yellowstone, Yosemite, and Big Bend, but it is mostly by luck, and, depending on how one approaches this grand hobby, it can be quite dangerous. The days of feeding the bears along the highways or in campgrounds are gone, and that means close-up photography is restricted, and now, because of some tragedies that have occurred in recent years, the feeding of all wildlife is prohibited or regulated in some fashion.

Photography enthusiasts must be cautioned about approaches into wildlife territory. As clumsy and awkward as the giant elephant seal appears at Channel Islands, it will attack any human who "threatens" its habitat. Seemingly calm and complacent grazing bison will turn and charge photographers who have wandered too close to a calf. Even a handout to a chipmunk in return for a pose risks a rabid bite.

In some cases it is advisable for the inexperienced not to attempt an expedition beyond park-recommended trails. In all instances the animals are wild. This is not the world of the nature film, where the cute and clever chipmunk performs before the camera, or where the moose calf or bear cub, as photogenic as it may be, walks blithely to the visitor for a handout unobserved by its parents. All national parks have rules and regulations on intentional or unintentional feeding of animals and they should be observed for the visitors' safety.

The cougar or mountain lion is the largest cat family member in North America and one of the most rarely seen.

A young great horned owl: the head is still covered in fuzzy first-year plumage, and the feathery "horns" have yet to grow to full size.

Nature walks and other supervised park activities frequently provide excellent opportunities for seeing wildlife in national parks, some that would not otherwise be available. But one should know something about the quest before striking out with or without supervision. All park visitor centers and most contact stations have small bookstores operated by non-profit, educational organizations that provide an assortment of wildlife guides and literature. Frequently bird and mammal checklists are available for pennies. These books and folders will fill the gaps with illustrations, pertinent data on habitats, and identification characteristics. For example, the Yellowstone Library and Museum Association, Grand Canyon Natural History Association, Big Bend Natural History Association, and similar organizations, can be contacted in care of the park for mail-order catalogs. Knowing something about the park and its wildlife, to say nothing of safety tips, camping, activities, and facility information, all in advance, is always good planning. The Natural History Associations are there to help. Contact local national park offices for a list of those associated with the national parks.

Enjoy national park wildlife. Let the animals have their way. This is their home. They are an integral part of the parks' ecological system, interacting, as they always have, long before humans came into the picture. Disturbing the setting — feeding a chipmunk or a bird, or getting too close to take a picture — may not necessarily be breaking a rule or law, but it is a violation of nature, a disruption of the delicate balance between the animal and its inherent sense of survival. Your respect, at a distance, will ensure that the animals, to say nothing of the magnificent scenery, will be there for others to enjoy.

Below *Bison graze in the Yellowstone National Park. The species was almost extinct by 1872 when this first national park was created by Congress, becoming a major sanctuary in which the bison herds could be regenerated.*

Right Prairie dogs come out from their burrows to see if the coast is clear.

Below The moose grows its antlers anew each year. At first they are covered with hairy skin known as "velvet".

1

THE ENDANGERED: THREE GREAT AMERICAN ICONS

No one really knows how many bison, or buffalo as they are commonly called, roamed across North America before the European came. Some say 100 million; others estimate that there were 60 million, perhaps 75 million, and they were seen as far east and south as Georgia. One 1839 report claimed a herd covering 1350 square miles. By the mid-nineteenth century, however, gunpowder and rifles had been introduced into the American West, and the bison population dropped dramatically. As early as 1830 there were fewer than 40 million of this huge mammal remaining; a few years later it was reported that more than 100 000 hides were being taken out of one region each year. Still, herds were of impressive size. As late as 1873 one sighting in the Dakotas was estimated to cover 50 or more square miles.

It was neither nature nor the Native American that reduced the bison population, however, contrary to some accounts. Great herds could consume vast amounts of grass, literally thousands of tons, in a single day, forcing them to move constantly; but prairie grass regenerated quickly, providing a nearly inexhaustible source of food. Many of the bison succumbed to disease, drought, and savage winters, and, of course, some to the Indians who used the meat and hides for their own survival; but still some 20 million calves were born each year to replenish the stock.

It was something else that decimated this native mammal, a national madness that brought on one of the most shameful periods of our American history — the great slaughter of the American Indian and the American bison simultaneously. Some historians link the two; others are more prone to credit the frontiersmen with simply having gone berserk with fair game on the plains. Whatever it was, beginning with the great move to push the Indian across the West into captivity in 1830, the white man went after the bison. Without this mammal, so the federal government maintained, the American Indian was lost. He ate the meat, used the hide for clothing and shelter, made thread and rope from sinew and tools from bones, and he used the droppings as fuel;

Right *A bison in the snow in Yellowstone National Park. Its thick coat protects it from blizzards, but long-lying snow can cover the grass and cut off food supplies.*

Following pages *This "story without words" engraving of 1844 depicts Indian braves hunting bison, as they did for centuries without harm to stock numbers.*

without the bison, the very fiber of Native American life would be destroyed. The Indian could be subdued.

Whether it was such a deliberate plot or a commercial interest in bison by-products, as some have suggested, which led to the wholesale destruction of buffalo makes little difference. The railroads shipped back the hides, the army thrived on buffalo meat, millions of pounds of bones were ground into fertilizer, and the Indian began to dwindle away. By 1900 there were fewer than 1000 bison left in the United States, and only a few more than that in Canada. The bison, unique to America, was virtually gone. Only extraordinary measures saved the few for later generations to see.

There are apocryphal stories of Indians who saved a few calves from the great slaughter, meaning, of course, that today's herds come from those few. Be that as it may, by the time Yellowstone was declared a national park in 1872 the bison was nearly extinct. In fact, Yellowstone National Park became one of its major sanctuaries. The 500 living today in the park represent one of the few completely wild and free-ranging herds in North America. They roam at will, but rarely leave the park boundaries, and they seem to survive the harsh winters much the same as their ancestors did on the plains centuries ago.

There are small herds at Wind Cave National Park (about 350), Grand Teton National Park (about 300), Theodore Roosevelt National Park, and

Above *These bison in Yellowstone's Hayden Valley are part of a 500-strong herd that lives a free-ranging, near-natural life in the national park.*

Inset *Bison, like domestic cattle, keep their horns for life, and do not grow new ones annually.*

Above *Bison bull at Wind Cave National Park, licking the red mud for salt.*

Badlands National Park; Custer State Park, South Dakota; Fort Niobrara Wildlife Refuge, Nebraska; National Bison Range, Montana; Prince Albert National Park, Saskatchewan; Riding Mountain National Park, Manitoba; Sullys Hill National Game Preserve, North Dakota; Waterton Lake National Park, Alberta; Wood Buffalo National Park, Alberta; Wichita Mountains Wildlife Refuge, Oklahoma.

There is a total of about 30 000 bison surviving today, and they are easily visible in the national parks. They are among the most gregarious mammals on earth and are seen mostly in herds, rarely alone, although two- and three-year-old calves often group together to play. The bison has poor eyesight, but its senses of smell and hearing are keen, so caution should be used in trying to become acquainted. Distance and telephoto lenses are best for photographs. The bison stampedes quickly; it walks at 5 miles an hour, but can gallop at 35 miles an hour.

The bison is the largest terrestrial animal in North America. Its huge, dark brown head with shaggy mane and beard is one of the most common of America's images, along with the bald eagle and the American Indian. The male will weigh up to 2000 pounds, the female 1000 pounds, accounting for many losses when crossing frozen rivers and lakes. Many main highways across the west follow trails created by the enormous weight and immense numbers of bison. America has truly been marked by this legendary mammal.

In 1784 Benjamin Franklin wrote his daughter Sarah:

"I wish that the bald eagle had not been chosen as the representative of our country; he is a bird of bad moral character; he does not get his living honestly; you may have seen him perched on some dead tree, where, too lazy to fish for himself, he watches the labor of the fishing-hawk, and when that diligent bird has at length taken a fish, and is bearing it to his nest for the support of his mate and young ones, the bald eagle pursues him and takes it from him."

Franklin called the eagle a "rank coward" and suggested that the turkey would be a better choice for America's national symbol. Perhaps the eagle's social behavior leaves something to be desired, but Franklin had little support for the turkey, and the Continental Congress approved a seal with the bald eagle on June 20, 1782.

The United States was far from the first nation to adopt the eagle as its symbol. More than 5000 years ago the eagle was the guardian divinity of Lagash, a major city of southern Mesopotamia. To ancient Rome the eagle was a symbol of victory and its image was emblazoned on the legions' standards. Later, Christians adopted the eagle as symbolic of ascension. Charlemagne, Napoleon, and Peter the Great, and, until the days of the swastika, the German Empire and the German Republic all used the eagle as their emblem. And in the New World both the Indians of Mexico and North America revered the eagle for its impressive hunting capabilities.

Right A *soaring bald eagle displays its enormous wing span.*

Below *The bald eagle has a reputation for stealing food from other birds of prey, but here's one that has caught a fine salmon and won't need to play the highwayman.*

Left *The bald eagle is not bald, but has magnificent white head plumage and neck ruff.*

Right *The stick nest of a bald eagle pair, high in a pine tree. Each year the occupants add a few sticks, building up a vast pile.*

Below *The bald eagle appeared on the badge of two US moon missions: Apollo 16, and Apollo 11, the first landing.*

The bald eagle is native only to North America, but both the bald and the golden eagle are protected by law, and for good reason. Despite the nationwide prevalence of its image, most Americans have never seen a bald eagle in the wild, and chances of their doing so are growing increasingly remote. The eagle has become a victim of human progress and, unless something is done beyond mere protection by law, we may lose one of North America's most magnificent birds. Severe penalties have been handed down in recent years for the wanton killing of the eagle, accused of being the predator of sheep and other small farm animals. As many as 1000 eagles a year were being shot, some from airplanes in flight. The Bald Eagle Act of 1940 (16 USC 668-668d; 54 Stat. 250) made an attempt to end this, but subsequent amendments have strengthened the legislation and now the Act provides for protection of both the bald eagle and the golden eagle by prohibiting killing, taking possession, and commerce in such birds.

When settlers began to expand America from the east to the west there were as many as 75 000 bald eagles in our skies. No one counted, of course, but there were estimates of 25 000 and more. Almost immediately the eagle became the victim of that westward expansion. Bald eagles have few natural enemies; but man became a predator. The wilderness was cleared; tall nesting trees disappeared. Large populations moved and declined. Then came the killings, and the nest-robbing egg collectors, and still later, pesticides absorbed by fish and transmitted to the eagle. By the early 1970s fewer than 3000 bald eagles remained in the lower 48 states. Today the greatest number is in Alaska, perhaps as many as 50 000. It is listed as "endangered" in 43 of the lower 48 states and "threatened" in the remaining five.

The bald eagle is probably our most easily recognizable bird. Because of the vast commercial use of its image and some magnificent color photography in recent years, even the city-dweller would be hard-pressed to miss identifying the majestic white head, fierce yellow beak, and frightening black talons. Males generally measure nearly 3 feet from head to tail, weigh 8 to 10 pounds, and have a wingspread of 6½ feet. Females are larger and may reach 42 inches and weigh up to 14 pounds, with a wingspread of 8 feet.

The bald eagle has been sighted in a number of national parks, but is most common in Everglades, Glacier, Grand Teton, Kings Canyon, Sequoia, Wind Cave, Yellowstone and Yosemite. As with most of the rare wildlife, the chances of spotting a bald eagle are few without some orientation from park rangers. Generally nesting areas are known and with patience and good field glasses some visitors have luck. On the other hand bald eagles are unpredictable in flight patterns and periodically they are sighted in unaccustomed areas. Their usual habitats are along lakes, rivers, and marshes. Wherever seen, they are truly magnificent, and no one forgets the experience.

Right *Golden eagle chicks at four weeks old.*

Far right *A golden eagle's talons are covered in horny projections to get a good grip on the prey. This is a youngster's foot, as the white juvenile plumage and yellow skin show.*

Below right *A golden eagle tearing meat from a carcass left out for it by the park ranger.*

Below *Bald eagle soaring over Chilkat Valley, Alaska.*

While the buffalo stands alone as an American icon of the West and the bald eagle remains forever ensconced as the symbol of American freedom, the grizzly bear, once endangered, is probably this country's most popular and fascinating wild animal. The grizzly captured the imagination of the American public from the first reports of the Lewis and Clark expedition in 1806 — its ability to stand like a man, its height and weight, its incredible power, its fearlessness of humans. Today we know it as the most complex, the least understood, and, in recent years, the most controversial of mammals, all of which are the result of man's inability to cope with this huge, enigmatic creature of the past.

Bears in national parks conjure images of tourists feeding the intrepid mammals from the windows of their cars in Yellowstone and the Great Smokies. This was the black bear and certainly a familiar postcard picture. It is no more. In fact, it has been illegal to feed bears in national parks for over 80 years, but because it was so popular it became quite clear that the management of the bear population, particularly in Yellowstone and Glacier National Parks, required very serious consideration. Since 1873 only three people had fallen victim to grizzly bears in any of our national parks. Then in one day in August 1967 two young women were killed by grizzlies in Glacier National Park in two widely separated and totally unrelated incidents. The fate of bears in national parks changed that day.

The controversy over bear management in national parks has raged for decades and it will continue. How to control the bear population — both grizzly and black — after many years of their feeding at park dumping grounds; how to minimize dangerous conflicts with park visitors; how to encourage the bears to revert to their natural habitat.

Right Portrait of a grizzly. Its shaggy looks and fearless behaviour led nineteenth century scientists to name it Ursus horribilis, *"the horrible bear".*

Below Grizzly bear mother and cubs playing on a snow field in the Alaska range.

Above *The grizzly is strong enough to wade through rapids to catch salmon.*

Left *Black, brown and grizzly bears are primarily forest dwellers and their cubs are good tree climbers. These four black bear cubs live in Yellowstone National Park.*

These were very important questions that still have to be answered, though they remain as the basis of park policies. The grizzly still roams Yellowstone, Glacier, and Denali, and there are occasional encounters with humans; but slowly it is being moved back to the wilds and the chances of seeing one diminish.

Preparation is the best safety tip for anyone traveling into the Yellowstone or Glacier grizzly country. A little advance study may make the difference between a close encounter and no encounter at all.

The grizzly is yellowish-brown to black, often with silver-looking or white tipped hairs, giving it a "grizzled" appearance. Its most distinguishing features are a large hump over the shoulders and a concave or "dished-out" face. Its height at the shoulders is about $4\frac{1}{4}$ feet; standing on hind feet, it can measure an astounding 7 feet. Primarily nocturnal, the grizzly has a low, clumsy walk, swinging its head back and forth; when necessary, however, it can run as fast as a horse.

This animal has one primary concern in life — eating. Although classified, like all bears, as a carnivore, the grizzly is omnivorous. It will graze on grass, harvest berries and fruits, chew on bark, leaves, and wild plants, and, in addition to catching assorted mammals, reptiles, and insects, it is an expert fisherman and relishes salmon. It has a keen sense of smell and will find campers' food caches with little trouble. Rangers will tell you to tie food containers high in trees. Cubs can climb, but adult bears rarely ever attempt to go after humans or their food supplies in the trees. Of course, there is always the exception to the rule.

Unprovoked attacks are not common, but that is no reason to drop caution. While the situation has changed somewhat in the past few years, bears in national parks have lost their fear of man, and whether they are encountered in the campground or the wilderness they should be viewed as extremely dangerous, and from afar.

2

AMONG THE TREES

Yellowstone National Park has one of the largest variety of animals in the entire national park system, and while there are vast acres of forests that harbor the secret habitats of the black and grizzly bears, there are thousands of acres of open space where one has hardly to leave the automobile to see elk and moose. Because wildlife is such an integral part of Yellowstone, this is the perfect setting to explore those animals that scamper about the floors of the forests. Some live in the trees. Most derive their diet from the trees in one form or another.

Most park animals are nocturnal, active only at night, and rarely make a daytime appearance. Some are diurnal (active in daylight), however, and have learned to live with the daily stream of humans tramping over their territory. Perhaps the most common is the squirrel family. About 45 of the 60 North American species are found in national parks, and, with the exception of two species of flying squirrel, which are solely nocturnal, all are seen at one time or another.

The most prevalent is the chipmunk. Of the 21 North American species, 15 are seen quite readily, but it is extremely difficult, even for experts, to determine precisely which is which. Mammalogists have divided them into the eastern and the western chipmunk, and that's probably just as well for all of us. Chipmunks, however, are always identified as the only North American ground squirrel with a dark facial stripe, bordered by white stripes, running through the eye.

There are a dozen or so specific chipmunks that reside in our parks, and at Yellowstone there are two of the western species that are most prevalent — the Uinta and the least. The least chipmunk is one of the smallest, probably no more than $3\frac{1}{2}$ to $4\frac{1}{2}$ inches in the body and with a tail of about the same length, but, again, it is difficult to differentiate this little fellow from others unless they are sitting side by side, and the chances of that happening are about as great as seeing a mountain goat without a pair of field glasses. It seems hardly worth the time and trouble to try to identify these delightful little mammals; they're here and there so fast, it's much more fun just to watch them foraging.

Right The red squirrel is just one of eight North American tree squirrels. It lacks the cheek pouches of ground squirrels and looks leaner in the face.

There is one thing everyone should remember, however, and that is to use caution when attempting to feed the chipmunk. It's not a good idea to do it in a national park — "do not feed the animals" — but wherever, there is always the chance of a rabid bite. Chipmunks and other members of the squirrel family will indeed become brave enough to take a handout, but an unintentional and quick movement of the hand may frighten the animal, and it may defend itself with a nip on the hand.

The best parks for sighting the eastern chipmunk are Great Smoky Mountains and Shenandoah; the western chipmunk, and the several varieties thereof, in Bryce Canyon, Grand Canyon, Rocky Mountain, Sequoia, Yellowstone, and Yosemite. Voyageurs is the only national park where both the western and eastern species are found together.

Of the 18 species of ground squirrel 15 live in national parks. The golden-mantled and Cascade golden-mantled ground squirrels have a white stripe bordered with black on their sides and resemble large chipmunks. One other striped species is the thirteen-lined ground squirrel; it has 13 dark and light stripes running the length of its body. The antelope squirrel has a white stripe, but no black ones. Another means of identification is the length of tails. The Townsend, Richardson, Uinta, Belding, Columbia, spotted, and round-tailed ground squirrels all have tails less than 5 inches long. The Franklin, California ground, and the rock squirrels have long tails, more than 5 inches. The Arctic ground squirrel has a tail $3\frac{1}{2}$ to $5\frac{1}{2}$ inches long and is found only in Alaska.

Right When a chipmunk has food in its cheek pouches its face has a chubby look.

Far right Someone gave this ground squirrel a piece of candy: however, it is not a good idea to feed animals in the national parks.

Below right A red squirrel in late winter, before the buds have opened: it has been lucky enough to find a berry.

Below The least chipmunk pictured here about one-and-a-half times life size.

The ground squirrel, of whatever species, is so common and so adjusted to park visitors that sightings are frequent. One can hardly go any place without encountering a squirrel or chipmunk. Only three are found in Yellowstone: golden-mantled, Uinta ground, and the red squirrel. One or more members of the squirrel family are to be found in most every other park in the system. Arctic ground squirrel: Katmai, Denali; Townsend: Zion; Uinta: Grand Teton, Yellowstone; Belding: Kings Canyon, Lassen Volcanic, Sequoia, Yosemite; Columbian: Glacier; Richardson: Glacier, Rocky Mountain; rock: Arches, Big Bend, Bryce Canyon, Canyonlands, Capitol Reef, Carlsbad Caverns, Grand Canyon, Guadalupe Mountains, Mesa Verde, Petrified Forest, Zion; California: Crater Lake, Kings Canyon, Lassen Volcanic, Redwood, Sequoia, Yosemite; thirteen-lined: Badlands, Glacier, Theodore Roosevelt, Wind Cave; golden-mantled: Bryce Canyon, Capitol Reef, Crater Lake, Glacier, Grand Canyon, Grand Teton, Kings Canyon, Lassen Volcanic, Mesa Verde, Rocky Mountain, Sequoia, Yosemite; Cascade golden-mantled: Mount Rainier, North Cascades; spotted: Big Bend, Grand Canyon, Guadalupe Mountains, Petrified Forest; Harris' antelope: Grand

Below left *A display of agility – and stretchability – given by a gray squirrel in the branches of a pine tree.*

Below *Flying squirrel grips an acorn in a red oak: its furry gliding flaps are folded along its sides.*

Below right *The flying squirrel steers its course through the air by adjusting the position of the flaps.*

Canyon; white-tailed antelope: Arches, Canyonlands, Capitol Reef, Grand Canyon, Petrified Forest, Zion; Texas antelope: Big Bend, Carlsbad Caverns, Guadalupe Mountains.

Tree squirrels obviously nest and live in the trees and are most proficient in climbing and leaping; unlike their ground cousins, they do not have cheek pouches, but they do forage on the ground and even store food there. Seven of the eight North American species are found in national parks, and they are quite plentiful. The red and Douglas' squirrels are the most common and can usually be recognized by their noisy chatter, actually a means of marking their territory.

Red squirrel: Acadia, Bryce Canyon, Denali, Glacier Bay, Glacier, Grand Canyon, Grand Teton, Great Smoky Mountains, Isle Royale, Katmai, Mesa Verde, North Cascades, Rocky Mountains, Shenandoah, Voyageurs, Wind Cave, Yellowstone, Zion; Douglas': Crater Lake, Kings Canyon, Lassen Volcanic, Mount Rainier, North Cascades, Olympic, Redwood, Sequoia, Yosemite. Other species of tree squirrel are the gray, Western gray, Abert's, Fox, Arizona gray, and red-bellied, all of which inhabit national parks.

Another frequently-seen mammal group is the rabbit and hare family. Rabbits include the cottontail, brush, marsh, and swamp rabbits. The cottontails — eastern, desert, Nuttall's, and New England — are quite prevalent in parks, wherever there are grasses for them to feed on. The eastern cottontail is found mostly at Big Bend, Everglades, Great Smoky Mountains, Guadalupe Mountains, Hot Springs, Mammoth Cave, Shenandoah, and Wind Cave; the New England cottontail at Great Smoky Mountains and Shenandoah; Nuttall's cottontail at Canyonlands, Crater Lake, Grand Canyon, Lassen Volcanic, Mesa Verde, Rocky Mountain, Yellowstone, and Zion.

The life-span of a cottontail is relatively short, only about a year. They are preyed on by a large variety of birds and mammals, including hawks, foxes, and coyotes, and, of course, they breed rapidly, whatever the species. Normally the cottontail keeps its tail with the underside down; but when frightened, the tail goes up and the white underside acts as a warning to others.

The desert cottontail is seen in nearly every western park, including Arches, Badlands, Grand Canyon, Kings Canyon, Mesa Verde, Wind Cave, and Zion. The marsh rabbit is found only at Biscayne and Everglades and is one of the larger of the cottontails — about 18 inches. It lives in the wetlands and swims well, and it is probably the most frequently-seen mammal in the Everglades.

One difference between rabbits and hares is that the offspring of rabbits are born with their eyes closed and have little fur; hare offspring are born fully furred, with their eyes open, and are up and running within hours of birth. The jack rabbit is really a long-eared hare; "Jackass Rabbit" is the common name given to several species living in the western parks — Arches, Big Bend, Canyonlands, Grand Canyon, Sequoia, and Yosemite, for example. The long ears allow the hare to lose heat in warm climates; the southern species have longer ears than their northern cousins.

The snowshoe hare is found throughout the United States and is distinguished by the fact that during the summer it has a dark brown coat, but in winter it molts to pure white. The northern hare lives in Alaska and molts to white also, but it is larger than the snowshoe. The northern hare is seen only at Katmai; but the snowshoe is found at Acadia, Crater Lake, Denali, Glacier Bay, Glacier, Grand Teton, Isle Royale, Katmai, Lassen Volcanic, Mount Rainier, North Cascades, Olympic, Rocky Mountain, Voyageurs, Yellowstone, and Yosemite.

Top right The white-tailed jack rabbit is not a rabbit but a hare. Like the snowshoe hare, it molts into white fur for the winter.

Below right Uinta ground squirrels are seen in Yosemite and Grand Teton National Parks.

Below Eastern cottontail rabbit sunning itself near the burrow that it has taken over from a prairie dog.

Yellowstone and Grand Teton have the largest elk populations of any national park. It is the most common mammal in Yellowstone — about 20 000 in the summer months — and can be seen at Gibbon Meadow and Elk Park near Madison Junction, and in the winter at the Elk Refuge at Grand Teton. Along with the moose, mule and black-tailed deer, white-tailed deer, and the caribou, the elk is of the deer family and native to North America. Conspicuous by its size and magnificent antlers, the elk now lives mostly in the Rocky Mountain range and along the Pacific coast. The male may weigh from 600 to 1100 pounds and stand 5 feet at the shoulders. Its graceful antlers may reach another 4 to 5 feet and will often spread 6 feet across. The male has a shaggy mane and short tail, dark chestnut-brown head and neck, and greyish-brown sides and back.

Below Bull elk sparring in Yellowstone. Usually the weaker bull withdraws after a brief trial of strength, but injuries sometimes do occur and, on rare occasions, these can prove fatal.

The moose is the largest of the deer family and is at once majestic and dangerous. None of the deer species should be regarded as friendly and viewed nonchalantly, least of all the moose. The male weighs up to 1800 pounds and stands 7 feet or more at the shoulders. Its ungainly appearance belies the speed with which it can charge if provoked. Moose have been clocked at 35 miles an hour. There are some moose at Acadia, Denali, Grand Teton, North Cascades, and Voyageurs, but the most common parks for good sightings are Glacier, Isle Royale, and Yellowstone.

The caribou is the American "version" of the reindeer, the Old World species of deer that has been domesticated in northern Eurasia, but here they are found only in the Alaska parks — Katmai only in the winter, and on the tundra of Denali in the summer.

Left A *moose refreshing itself in a lake, its growing antlers a glorious flame red.*

Right A *bull caribou in spring: its antlers have just reached full size and the last strips of velvet are about to fall.*

Right inset A *caribou silhouetted against the twilight at Denali National Park and Preserve, Alaska.*

Below A *moose cow and her young: these two are about one month old and need constant maternal supervision.*

Left The mule deer, seen in 27 national parks.
It is intermediate in size between the moose
and the white-tailed deer.

Below A moose running in Yellowstone. This
horse-sized member of the deer family can charge
at 35 miles per hour.

The most common deer in national parks, and seemingly the most tame, are the mule and black-and white-tailed. Although there are great similarities, it is generally accepted that the black-tailed deer is a subspecies of the mule deer. The large mule-like ears give the species its name. The mule deer is found mostly in the western United States, whereas the white-tailed deer is mainly an eastern species.

The mule deer stands about 3 to $3\frac{1}{2}$ feet at the shoulder. Its fur is reddish-brown in the summer and greyish in the winter, and the tail tip is black. Male antlers fork into two nearly equal branches. The mule deer is readily seen in Arches, Badlands, Big Bend, Bryce Canyon, Canyonlands, Capitol Reef, Carlsbad Caverns, Crater Lake, Glacier, Grand Canyon, Grand Teton, Guadalupe Mountains, Kings Canyon, Lassen Volcanic, Mesa Verde, Mount Rainier, North Cascades, Olympic, Petrified Forest, Redwood, Rocky Mountain, Sequoia, Roosevelt, Wind Cave, Yellowstone, Yosemite, and Zion.

The white-tailed deer takes its name from the white underside of the tail, and it is much smaller than the mule deer, measuring $2\frac{3}{4}$ feet at the shoulder. It is now the most abundant hoofed mammal in North America, seen mostly in the early morning hours at Acadia, Badlands, Big Bend, Crater Lake, Everglades, Great Smoky Mountains, and Voyageurs.

The pronghorn, quite numerous at Yellowstone, is sometimes called the "American antelope" or *Antilocapra*, meaning "antelope goat," although it is neither antelope nor goat and not even closely related. Rather, it is the sole remnant of an ancient family dating back to some 20 million years ago. It has the distinction of being the fastest mammal in the American continent — which certainly would seem to relate it to the antelope — but it is also probably the most mysterious since so little is known about its beginnings.

Below *White-tailed deer browsing on spring foliage in Glacier National Park, Montana.*

Until very recently ruminants with horns that were not sheep, goats, or oxen were considered antelopes. Horns, unlike antlers, are not normally branched and grow throughout an animal's life. The pronghorn is the only animal in the world with branched horns that are shed. It is uniquely American, then, and a uniquely beautiful animal.

The pronghorn is deer-like in appearance, 35 to 41 inches at the shoulders, weighing 100 to 125 pounds, with a pale tan or reddish-tan upper body; its sides, chest, belly, inner legs, and rump patch are white. Its speed is something to behold: it has been clocked at 70 miles an hour, and will turn and sprint at the least threat to its safety, thus making it extremely difficult to observe. Park rangers know where herds graze and can guide visitors. Attempts to track alone without knowledge of their habits generally result in failure.

Left A pronghorn looks round for pursuers: a quick 70-mile-an-hour sprint should easily shake them off.

Below This trumpeter swan has migrated north in spring to breed in Alaska. It constructs a vast nest of dried reed stems on which to lay and incubate the eggs.

Yellowstone is a collection of great natural wonders; but sometimes its wildlife is dwarfed by the immensity of Old Faithful or the Grand Canyon of the Yellowstone. Everyone knows of the elk, the moose, and the bear, but this park has played a great role in the survival of other animals. The trumpeter swan, for example, owes its survival to protection measures taken in Yellowstone 50 years ago. Yellowstone has the only white pelican breeding colony in any national park. And there are great blue herons, sandhill cranes, ravens, bald eagles, golden eagles, Canada geese, and Harlequin ducks.

There are not many reptiles and amphibians in Yellowstone; occasionally a rattlesnake, bullsnake, or garter snake will be spotted by a visitor, and salamanders have been reported migrating from one lake to another. More interesting is the attraction at Fishing Bridge on the Yellowstone where every summer thousands of visitors watch fish in their wild state — Yellowstone cutthroat trout, fine-spotted Snake River cutthroat trout, Montana grayling, mountain sucker, longnose sucker, mottled sculpin, Utah chub, and speckled dace, to name a few.

Inset left *Silhouetted against the dawn are ten great blue herons. This heronry is on the banks of the Carson River, Nevada.*

Below left *A small flock of pelicans patrolling a quiet stretch of water.*

Right *Part of a formation flight by a flock of Canada geese over Hayden Valley in Yellowstone National Park.*

Below *A harlequin drake in Glacier National Park, Montana: his plumage is a mosaic of green, brown, black and white, brilliantly complemented by the fiery red, yellow and black of his eyes and bill.*

3
ALONG THE SHORES

Along the national seashores, and in the marshes of the Everglades, live some of the most ancient of North American wildlife — the alligator, gray whale, dolphin, porpoise, manatee, northern elephant seal, and the California sea lion. While park boundaries seldom go beyond the shore lines, these great mammals have long been considered a part of the park system, if only because they provide many hours of pleasure for visitors. For example Cabrillo National Monument at Point Loma, San Diego, California, is a historic site commemorating the landing of the Spanish explorer; one of the main attractions at the park, however, is watching the gray whale as it migrates north and south in season just off the coast. Harbor seals live in the waters and along the rocky ledges at Acadia National Park in Maine. And at Channel Islands National Park just off the Pacific Coast at Los Angeles the great northern elephant seal and the California sea lion are as much a part of the park as the gray fox and rabbit that scoot about on the land.

The largest and most feared reptile in North America is the American alligator, *Alligator mississippiensis*. Nearly extinct not many years ago because of poaching for its hide, the alligator is now protected and is making a comeback in southern Florida and the Everglades. They are readily seen along the roads and trails of the park — at Shark Valley and along the Anhinga Trail — and are easily distinguished from the smaller spectacled cayman and American crocodile. The alligator measures from 6 feet to 19 feet; the crocodile from 5 to 7 feet; the cayman between 4 and 9 feet. And, if not seen, the male alligator can certainly be heard. During the breeding season the adult produces a throaty, bellowing roar that can be heard over great distances, adding to the eeriness of the nights in the Everglades.

The alligator is an important link in the ecological chain in its environment, and it has well earned its title "Keeper of the Everglades". The "gator holes" it digs in the limestone bed of the Everglades serve as oases in the dry winter season, holding fresh water for other creatures.

Right *Bottle-nosed dolphin swimming upright in a near-human pose. Dolphins are the easiest cetaceans (whale relatives) to see from the US coasts.*

46

Here the "king of beasts" hibernates in the winter and feeds on fish, small mammals, birds, turtles, snakes, and frogs. In the spring predators and prey leave the holes and begin the cycle of life over again.

There are ten species of hair seals in North America, but only three are found in national parks — the harbor, gray, and elephant seal. These mammals differ from fur seals and sea lions in having no external ear, only a small opening, and in not being able to rotate their hind flippers forward as fur seals and sea lions can.

The harbor seal is the smallest of the species and can be found on both the Atlantic and Pacific coasts at Acadia, Channel Islands, Glacier Bay, Katmai, Olympic, and Redwood, and along most other coastal parks except Biscayne and Everglades. It is about 5 feet long and has a gray coat with black spots. The gray seal is larger, about 10 feet in length, and has a gray coat without spots. It is found only at Acadia in Maine. The elephant seal is found only along the Pacific coast — Channel Islands, Olympic, and Redwood — and is the largest of the species, reaching as much as 20 feet in length and weighing up to 8000 pounds. The male is distinguished by an elephantlike trunk that protrudes out and down over the mouth.

Seals have been hunted for their skins for centuries, but the elephant seal was nearly exterminated for its blubber. At one time there were only 20 living on Guadalupe Island off the coast of Baja California in Mexico. Now protected by law, the current population is estimated at 40 000. Mostly nocturnal, the elephant seal can be seen during the day basking in the sun. It feeds at night on squid and fish and can dive more than 200 feet and stay submerged for a half-hour.

Right *Today, alligators are readily seen in the Everglades. When the weather is fine they haul themselves out onto dry, open banks to bask in the sunshine.*

Below *Alligator emerging from the swamp.*

48

Males feel threatened by humans walking near them and have been known to attack, yet a person crawling on hands and knees could move about without much danger. Neither method for getting acquainted with this huge mammal is advised.

Fur seals and sea lions are known as "eared seals" as distinguished from the earless or hair seals. Other than the small but conspicuous external ear, the eared seals can rotate their hind flippers forward and are able to walk in a quadrupedal fashion. The northern fur seal, or the Alaskan fur seal, is the most sought after in the fur trade because of a dense and velvety underfur. Males are about $7\frac{1}{4}$ feet long and weigh about 600 pounds, the females about $4\frac{1}{2}$ feet and 135 pounds. In late May and early June they assemble in large groups on the beaches of the Pribilof Islands of Alaska where the female gives birth. In November the

Below A scene in an elephant seal colony on the Pacific coast. Three of the cows (females) are having an argument, but the rest are happy to lie still and let it all blow over.

Inset A cow elephant seal guarding a youngster. It may not necessarily be her own, as the young are nursed collectively.

families migrate some 6000 miles to winter off the California coast, generally on the beaches and rocks of Channel Islands and Redwood National Parks. Their fur is still in demand, but by agreement with the several countries hunting in the open seas, the United States has been given custody, and harvesting of select males controls the population at about one million, with about 50 000 captured for the trade each year.

The Guadalupe fur seal is small and lighter and still somewhat scarce, breeding only on Guadalupe Island in Mexico. A few males journey to San Miguel in the Channel Islands each summer.

The California sea lion is the familiar trained seal of the circus and is a common species along the California coast, especially at Channel Islands where there is a resident population. The male is 7 feet long and weighs about 600 pounds, the female slightly smaller.

Main picture *Water streams off the tail flukes of a gray whale as it flips its tail above the surface before diving. For a sighting like this, try Cabrillo National Monument.*

Left *Gray whales are too large to leap like dolphins, but they can swim upright to get a view above the surface.*

There are some 44 species of whale, dolphin, and porpoise, most of which are infrequently seen. Only the migrating gray whale is predictable. For example, of the ten species of the goose-beaked whale, only one has been sighted from a national park, at Redwood. Sperm whales are sometimes seen from Olympic and Redwood. Many of the 20 species of dolphin and porpoise are frequently seen from the coast, but only ten have been sighted from park areas. The bottle-nosed dolphin is frequently spotted around Biscayne and Everglades, but less often along the Pacific Coast. Pilot whales can be seen from Everglades and Biscayne along the Atlantic, and Redwood, Olympic, and Channel Islands along the Pacific. The white-sided dolphin is occasionally spotted from Channel Islands and from Redwood and Olympic.

Gray whale watching is one of the most popular activities at several Pacific coast parks, including Channel Island, Redwood, and Olympic, but most notably at Cabrillo National Monument, an urban park that attracts visitors from San Diego. Telescopes have been installed along the cliff at Point Loma for viewing the migration out to sea.

The gray whale is a rather remarkable mammal and probably derives its popularity from being possibly the finest example of human interest and protection. In 1925 there were as few as 300 gray whales in existence, nearly the entire population having been killed off by whalers. International agreement for protection prevented its total annihilation just in time, however, and by 1960 an estimated 6000 made the annual migration. By the early 1980s gray whales exceeded the estimated population of the mid-nineteenth century.

It must be remembered that sighting any of these marine mammals is by chance and generally achieved only with an experienced eye or the assistance of park rangers and good field glasses. A little knowledge of precisely what one is looking for helps. Whale watching has become a major park theme at Cabrillo, where the Cabrillo Historical Association offers some excellent literature.

Varieties of whale can be observed at parks as follows: hump-backed whale: Acadia, Channel Islands, Glacier Bay, Redwood; blue whale: Channel Islands; gray whale: Cabrillo National Monument, Channel Islands, Olympic; killer whale: Channel Islands, Glacier Bay; common pilot whales: Acadia, Everglades, Olympic; Pacific white-sided dolphin: Channel Islands, Olympic, Redwood; Dall's porpoise: Channel Islands, Glacier Bay, Redwood.

It would be unforgivable to move on without acknowledging one of the least attractive, yet rare sea mammals found in any of our park areas, albeit only two, Biscayne and Everglades. After all, it was the first uniquely American mammal seen by Christopher Columbus; he called it a mermaid, but had to admit that it was not as attractive as anticipated. It was the lowly manatee, or as known by its least attractive name, the sea cow.

Today the manatee is a rare species, protected, and, perhaps, returning from near extinction, but it is an extremely fragile aquatic mammal found in a limited area around Florida. Almost prehistoric in appearance, the manatee may weigh up to 1400 pounds and measure 8 to 12 feet in length. Sightings are rare, but park rangers at Biscayne and Everglades can help with general locations.

Right A manatee feeding on sea-bed vegetation. Seaweeds and marine grasses are their chief food. The manatees also swim up rivers, feeding on underwater plants.

Below A group of manatees like this would be a prize sighting off the coast of Florida. They may not be beautiful but they are harmless and very trusting if you meet them face to face.

Once limited to the sea in the Hawaiian Islands, the Hawaiian goose, or nene, is one of those formerly almost extinct animals the National Park Service so proudly claims is coming back. Originally there may have been only 15 birds native to Hawaii; scientists estimate that perhaps 70 evolved from those before humans arrived. The most famous was the nene, pronounced "ney-ney." Descended from the Canada goose at some point through the centuries, the nene has evolved into a land bird, losing much of its webbing in the feet, and learning to live on sparsely vegetated lava flows. Now a ground-nesting bird, the nene was nearly wiped out when humans introduced rats and mongooses to the islands, and then went on hunting sprees. By 1951 there were only 33 known birds in existence, but the National Park Service, along with help from conservation agencies, has brought this magnificent bird back and it will now survive.

Above Close-up of the feet of the Hawaiian goose or nene. Long ago, when geese first took to the water, they evolved webbed feet for swimming. The Hawaiian goose has returned to dry land and is not a swimmer. Evolution has continued, and the bird has begun to lose its webs.

Left A family of Hawaiian geese in a wildfowl refuge.

4

SUPREME SURVIVORS: THE CARNIVORES

We look at carnivores, flesh-eating mammals, as the supreme survivors, and perhaps under normal circumstances they are. But the national parks and some wildlife refuges are the last bastions for the carnivores, for, in fact, they are the group of mammals most exploited by man, and in our lifetime we may well see the extinction of some species. The fox, mink, bobcat, badger, ermine, skunk and marten have been extensively hunted and trapped for their fur; the wolf, bear, coyote, and mountain lion, all of which feed on farm livestock, have been nearly wiped out; others, like the ferret, are rapidly disappearing because so is their chief source of food, the prairie dog. National parks offer some protection and, although most of the carnivores are nocturnal and secretive, a few can be seen during the day.

The *Carnivora* families found in national parks are the cat (mountain lion, bobcat, lynx); weasel (ermine, weasel, marten, fisher, ferret, skunk, badger, wolverine, otter, mink); dog (fox, wolf, coyote); bear (black, grizzly, polar); raccoon (raccoon, ringtail, coati); and the sea lion and hair seal families. (Several of these have been reviewed elsewhere in this text.) All these families are distinguished by their large, sabrelike canine teeth, and, of course, the characteristic of eating flesh, but some are omnivorous and also eat berries, fruit, and other vegetation such as leaves, bark, roots and underground tubers.

At one time it was the policy of the federal government to get rid of the coyote; indeed a campaign for total elimination was launched. Ironically, of the wild dog family, it is the coyote that has survived and multiplied and is found in 30 of our 48 national parks. In fact today the coyote roams areas of this country in which it had never been seen before, mating with domestic dogs and red and gray wolves, and eating almost any and everything. One reason for its survival is it is one of the most easily adaptable of our North American mammals. It has been known to eat 56 species of animal and 28 species of plant, not to mention other items fit only for the proverbial billygoat.

Right A *bobcat in winter, looking like a larger and more powerful version of the wild cat. It is present in Yellowstone, but rarely seen.*

58

A wolf calling to the rest of its pack. There is no shortage of wolves in the national parks, but this may be no bad thing. Naturalists these days believe the animal has an undeservedly bad reputation.

Above left *Raccoon mother carrying her baby at a trot.*

Below left *Mink with its prey: the bird it has caught is a grackle.*

Right *Ermine at the entrance to its den in Hayden Valley, Yellowstone. Its white fur has been prized by hunters for so long that the animal could not have survived without protection laws and the national parks.*

Below *American marten in its normal habitat, a pine wood.*

Coyotes generally are 3 to $4\frac{1}{2}$ feet long, with a 16-inch bushy tail, and they weigh from 18 to 44 pounds. Their coats vary from brownish- to reddish-gray (darker at higher altitudes), but today it is extremely difficult to determine a true coyote from a hybridization of the red wolf by size or color. The coyote has interbred with both the red and the gray wolf and so there is great similarity in their appearance.

The true red wolf is nearly extinct now and probably does not exist in any national park, unless in the form of a hybrid red wolf-coyote. The gray wolf survives, however, and is one of the most fascinating mammals ever studied in North America. It is found at Bryce Canyon, Denali, Glacier Bay, Glacier, Katmai, North Cascades, and Voyageurs. Denali is the only park in which there is a good chance of seeing wolves, but the one national park where the gray wolf plays an important role in the ecological system is Isle Royale. Here it has been the subject of extensive study in its relationship with the island's other major inhabitant, the moose. The Isle Royale Natural History Association can provide several excellent publications detailing these studies.

The wolf, like the grizzly bear, has been the subject of great controversy during the past few years. Barry Lopez's **Of Wolves and Men** (Charles Scribner's Sons, 1978) has gone far in presenting a new perspective on the relationship of wolves and humans. The wolf is the largest of the wild dogs, weighing up to 175 pounds and measuring $6\frac{1}{2}$ feet from nose to tail, and ranges in color from grayish or brownish to all white and all black.

Five of the six North American species of fox are found in national parks — red, kit, swift, gray, and insular gray fox. The most common is the red fox, found at Acadia, Bryce Canyon, Canyonlands, Capitol Reef, Crater Lake, Denali, Everglades, Glacier Bay, Glacier, Grand Teton, Hot Springs, Isle Royale, Katmai, Kings Canyon, Lassen Volcanic, Mammoth Cave, Mesa Verde, Mount Rainier, North Cascades, Rocky Mountain, Sequoia, Shenandoah, Theodore Roosevelt, Voyageurs, Yellowstone, and also Zion.

Although plentiful, sighting red fox is chancy. Mostly active at night, it is sometimes spotted in the early morning hours along streams and in grassy areas searching for rodents, one of its main sources of food. It weighs about 15 pounds and is $3\frac{1}{2}$ feet long. Its color ranges from reddish-yellow to silver body and tail, with a white belly and black feet. Traditionally a chicken thief, the fox also controls the rodent population.

The gray fox is a similar size to the red fox, but its color is mostly all grizzled gray, with a black stripe down the top of the tail; the belly and neck are rust-colored and the throat is white. The smaller insular gray fox is found only on San Miguel, Santa Rosa, and Santa Cruz of Channel Islands National Park.

Below left *Coyote digging a lair in loose earth. This successful hunting species has interbred with its fellow carnivore, the wolf.*

Left A red fox, wet from the rain, in Denali National Park.

Below A pair of coyotes consume a dead elk in Yellowstone National Park. What they leave will be more than enough for the crows.

Of the four species of bear in North America, only the polar bear is not found in any national park. The black bear ranges from Acadia in the east to Glacier Bay in Alaska. The smallest of North American bears, the black bear weighs up to 600 pounds and measures about 6 feet in length. Although its coat is black in the east, some western species are shades of cinnamon and may have the same coloration as the grizzly or brown bear. But there is no problem in distinguishing the black bear from the grizzly: the facial profile is decidedly different, an almost straight nose as opposed to the grizzly's dished-out look. And the black bear stands only about 3 feet at the shoulder. Although the black bear does not have the reputation of the grizzly, it is still considered dangerous and extreme caution should be used if one is sighted. The largest populations are found in Glacier, Sequoia, Shenandoah, Great Smoky Mountains, Yellowstone, and Yosemite.

Left *A gray fox hunts in a snowy field at sunset.*

Below *Black bear in Yellowstone, showing its straight-topped snout. Although it is not large by bears' standards, the black bear is over three times the weight of a man.*

5
RIVERS AND DESERTS

Few mammals have had as much impact on American history as the beaver. Certainly the bison played a role in the exploration of the West — it was there when the European arrived, providing food and hides for the natives as well as the explorer — and the horse and ox were instrumental in building farmlands across the nation, but it was the beaver that led the white man across the Appalachians into the unknown wilderness of the nineteenth century. The search for beaver pelts is attributed by many historians as the factor contributing most to the exploration of the American West. The fur was in constant demand for robes and coats, clothing trims, and top hats — called "beavers" — which became fashionable in European capitals and in the few urban areas of the east coast United States. Unregulated beaver trapping created great financial empires; some of America's more wealthy families can attribute their "old money" to vast profits from the trade in beaver skins.

Originally found throughout North America, from the Arctic treeline to the Mexican border, with the exception of the Florida peninsula and some areas in the desert southwest, the beaver had nearly died out by 1900. Regulated trapping and a decline in the use of pelts has saved the beaver from extinction.

Most mammals will alter their environment to some degree, if by nothing more than burrowing into the ground or constructing a nest, but the beaver changes things in grand style. Damming streams and small rivers with trees and branches seems harmless enough, but beaver lodges 7 feet high and 30 feet in diameter have been found, some altering the landscape permanently. Much of this work is done at night, or in areas not disturbed by humans, in early daylight or early dusk, and so beavers are seldom seen in the parks. They are found in Arches, Big Bend, Bryce Canyon, Canyonlands, Capitol Reef, Denali, Glacier, Grand Canyon, Grand Teton, Great Smoky Mountains, Isle Royale, Katmai, Mesa Verde, Mount Rainier, North Cascades, Olympic, Redwood, Rocky Mountain, Theodore Roosevelt, Voyageurs, Yellowstone, and Yosemite.

Top right *A beaver at the waterside, showing its round, flat tail.*

Middle right *Beaver swimming: the powerful tail is such a good propeller that the forepaws are not needed for swimming.*

Far right top *A beaver's work — nearly through now.*

Right *Beaver dam in Denali National Park: the result of patient industry.*

The river otter is another mammal that lives near or beside the water, much the same as the beaver — in fact, it sometimes lives in abandoned beaver lodges — and, like the beaver, its beautiful and luxurious fur is considered quite valuable. Nearly extinct just a few years ago, it is now protected and, as a species, should survive. The river otter is a large, rather streamlined, aquatic weasel with a thick neck, small eyes, prominent whiskers, short legs, and a long, heavy tail. It is completely at home in water and is a fast swimmer, propelling itself with its webbed feet and using its muscular tail as a scull. The river otter is found at Acadia, Denali, Everglades, Glacier Bay, Glacier, Grand Canyon, Grand Teton, Great Smoky Mountains, Isle Royale, Katmai, Lassen Volcanic, North Cascades, Olympic, Redwood, Theodore Roosevelt, Voyageurs, and Yellowstone.

Left River otter doing the backstroke: this is in play — for fishing, he flips over and swims faster.

Right Since the muskrat is a plant-eater it does not compete with the beaver for fish, so the two are always good neighbors.

Below Reenacting an old fable? Two desert dwellers of the American southwest: a desert cottontail and desert tortoise, both heading for the shade.

Evidence of the aquatic muskrat is more likely to be seen than the muskrat itself, although if all is quiet and there are not many people around, occasionally at dusk one can spot a muskrat swimming in a pond or lake. It is about a foot long, with another foot of tail, and weighs about 4 pounds. It is smaller than the beaver, but oddly enough it can be found housekeeping along with the larger animal, sometimes side by side in the same pond. It prefers a different diet from the beaver's — sedges, cattail stems, grasses, reeds — and its houses are built of the same kind of things, with nest chambers and underwater entrances. The round-tailed muskrat, about half the size of the regular muskrat, is found only at the Everglades. The other is found at Acadia, Arches, Canyonlands, Capitol, Reef, Denali, Glacier, Grand Teton, Great Smoky Mountains, Isle Royale, Katmai, Lassen Volcanic, Mammoth Cave, Mesa Verde, Olympic, Rocky Mountain, Shenandoah, Theodore Roosevelt, Voyageurs, Yellowstone, and Yosemite.

Left *Red-legged tarantula warming up in the sunlight.*

Below *Arizona's own variety of the collared peccary, burrowing down into desert sand.*

Following page *Brazilian free-tailed bats leaving Carlsbad caverns at dusk. Amazingly, there are always enough insects to sustain this massive population.*

The desert seems such an inhospitable place that the vast number of mammals, birds, and reptiles that survive the heat and barren land is astonishing. Some are the same animals found in other parts of the country, adapted to the harsher environment. The chipmunk, ground squirrel, and cottontail, for example, are simply designed in color and thickness of fur to cope with a different ecological system. There are a few animals that live only in the desert southwest — the armadillo and the desert tarantula, for example — but for the most part, the parks of the southwest are populated with mule deer (called the desert mule deer), black bear, beaver, bighorn sheep, bobcat, coyote, and elk.

At Big Bend in one of the most remote regions of Texas, there are two kinds of deer — the diminutive del Carmen white-tail deer in the Chisos mountains, and the larger desert mule deer at the lower elevations, seen frequently along the roads eating grass. Both are prey to the mountain lion (or "panther" in Texas), which has made a remarkable return following years of predator control.

The piglike collared peccary is a mean-looking critter, although not particularly dangerous to humans, and roams the park freely in herds of ten and twenty.

There are coyote and black bear at Big Bend, but they are seldom seen, although the mournful howl of the coyote can be heard at night. But while one is attempting to catch the elusive deer or coyote on the horizon with field glasses, scampering across the ground nearby may be a scorpion or tarantula, or perhaps one of 30 species of snake or 21 species of lizard.

Despite its bad press the tarantula is not really dangerous. Its venom is no more poisonous than a bee's, and it shies from attacking humans. Its image has been so well ingrained in our minds that it is quite easy to spot; the body is gray to dark-brown, the abdomen is brownish-black, and the leg span is four inches. During fall and winter months, when temperatures at high elevations drop significantly, tarantulas of all sizes can be seen on roadways basking in the morning sun.

The desert tortoise is an endangered species and is found only at Big Bend. It has a domed, horn-brown shell and round, stumpy hind legs. It can be spotted in the mornings and evenings eating grass, and like all tortoises, it crosses the highways "to get to the other side". Use caution when driving in all parks, but particularly where roads are just another human intrusion into the animals' world.

The Grand Canyon rattlesnake, one of four kinds at Big Bend, varies in size and color, being 1 to 4 feet long and with brownish blotches down the midline of the back, edged with dark brown or black and often surrounded by light colors.

West Texas specialties are the Trans-Pecos rat snake and the gray-banded king snake. Watch where you step and put your hands anyplace in the park and there will be no problem. Snakes are likely to be more frightened of you than you are of them.

Big Bend is a bird watcher's heaven. Several hundred species have been sighted. There is always the humorous roadrunner, which does occasionally take to the wing, the endangered peregrine falcon, and the Lucifer hummingbird and Colima warbler, which are not found in any other place in the country.

With the exception of the omnipresent kaibab squirrel on the north rim and the Abert squirrel on the south rim, and an occasional mule deer, wildlife at the Grand Canyon seems sparse. That image may well be the result of intent concentration on the magnificent scenery blotting out almost everything else. It is not surprising to hear visitors claim the only animals they saw at Grand Canyon were the mules carrying tourists down the trail.

In fact the Grand Canyon teems with all kinds of secretive animals, including the spotted skunk, badger, bobcat, desert cottontail, elk, mountain lion, Uinta chipmunk, and an occasional black bear. One must remember, however, that all of these do not live in the canyon. The south rim and the north rim, even though ecologically different from each other, provide forested areas for much of the park's wildlife.

Changes in the elevation from the Colorado River to the plateau (or the rims) are drastic in terms of plant and animal life. From the floor of the canyon, a 1000-foot increase in elevation is equivalent in climatic change to moving north 300 miles without increasing altitude. Inevitably there are several different life zones, and appropriate plants and animals to match. They begin at the river level and end at the high elevation of the north rim, and include the river otter along the Colorado and the wild turkey of the plateau.

Of all the canyon's wildlife, however, perhaps the most fascinating is the squirrel that got separated from itself, in a manner of speaking. The Kaibab squirrel, found only on the north rim, is very closely related to the Abert squirrel, found on the south rim. As far as scientists can figure, the Colorado River, cutting through the plateau, separated members of the original species. When it was impossible to cross the barrier, the two squirrels developed their own characteristics suitable to their own habitats, one becoming a subspecies of the other. The Kaibab squirrel is large, with tasseled ears and a white, bushy tail and black belly. The Abert squirrel is similar except the tail is black and the belly is white. Needless to say, both are equally attractive.

A few of the other animals living in the desert are: the deer mouse, the most common (in the southwest) of the 100 species of rats or mice in North America, a 5- to 8-inch, grayish to reddish-brown mouse that burrows in the ground at Arches, Bryce Canyon, Grand Canyon, Guadalupe Mountains, Mesa Verde, and Zion; Merriam's kangaroo rat, the smallest of the kangaroo rats, distinctive for giving itself a sand or dust bath to keep its fur from matting, found at Arches, Big Bend, Canyonlands, Grand Canyon, Mesa Verde, and Zion; the great horned owl, that indomitable creature that lives in trees, crevices, and cliffs at Big Bend, Bryce Canyon, Carlsbad Caverns, Grand Canyon, Guadalupe Mountains, Mesa Verde, Petrified Forest, and Zion.

And one of the more fascinating mammals, and the chief attraction at Carlsbad Caverns, is the Brazilian free-tailed bat. Each summer evening at sundown, and for about an hour thereafter, about 300 000 bats swirl out of this immense cave, devour about three tons of unsuspecting insects flying around the New Mexico night, and, at dawn, dive back into the dark depths of Carlsbad. This bat is the most common type in the southwest, with an estimated population of 100 million. Like all bats, it is a truly remarkable mammal. It operates its nightly foray on sonarlike radar — much more accurate than sight, it is said — and detects the insects in mid-air.

One cannot leave the southwest parks without a brief mention of the wild burros of Grand Canyon, although they can hardly be classified as wildlife and certainly have no place in Grand Canyon's natural history. Descendants of the burros used by miners to haul out ore from the canyon many years ago, the burros have in recent years become the subject of great controversy. Left behind to run wild, they have through the years destroyed a great deal of the canyon's vegetation, thus, in the chain reaction, causing much soil erosion. Between 1924 and 1969 the National Park Service eliminated 3000 of them, but then had to stop because of public pressure. The same happened in the early 1980s, when once more an attempt was made to mass exodus the burros, this time with considerably more success; but the controversy over this strange and seemingly unwanted animal goes on.

6

HIGH IN THE MOUNTAINS

Among the rarest and most cherished wildlife sightings in the mountain parks are the mountain goats in Glacier, and the Dall's and mountain, or bighorn, sheep at Denali. Sure-footed climbers have the greatest advantage, for all three of these animals range at the highest and most rocky elevations. Even then it is only the most fortunate and skilled of photographers that manage a few good pictures each year.

The mountain goat is not a true goat, but rather belongs to a family known as goat-antelopes, which includes the chamois of Europe and Asia Minor. While the horns of a true goat sweep up and back and are tightly spiraled like a corkscrew, the mountain goat's horns curve back slightly and are nearly smooth. Its coat is pure white and its chin beard is an extension of a throat mane rather than the "whiskers" of a true goat. From a distance, these characteristics resemble those of the Dall's sheep, and many viewers can be misled. The mountain goat is found only at Glacier Bay, Glacier, and Mount Rainier.

Active in the morning and evening, and sometimes during moonlight, the mountain goat feeds on grasses, sedges, and other green plants in summer, on woody plants in winter, and generally at high altitudes and along rocky ledges. Its hooves are adapted with rubbery soles and sharp outer rims that grip and provide traction on steep and smooth surfaces. Even though it seems that this beautiful mammal moves with ease and grace across sheer cliffs, it has been known to lose its footing and fall to its death. Rock slides and avalanches account for the greatest number of deaths, but the mountain goat does fall prey to the golden eagle and the cougar.

North America's two species of wild sheep differ in color and the conformation of horns, but only slightly in size. Dall's sheep is the northern species in Alaska, where they are white, and British Columbia, where they may be gray to black; the mountain or bighorn lives from British Columbia to Mexico and from California to the Rocky Mountain range, where they are generally dark brown. The most distinctive feature of both is their horns. Those of the Dall's sheep form a corkscrew-like

Right Mountains are a world apart from other types of habitat, and many of the animals that live there are specialists, such as the perfectly adapted mountain goat.

Inset The mountain goat is related to the chamois but has a longer, woollier coat.

Above A *bobcat lies in wait for prey in its rock den.*

Above left *Dall sheep ram. Dall sheep are the northern of our two species of wild sheep and are seen only at Denali. The bighorn is the southern species.*

Below left *The nine-foot long mountain lion or cougar is large enough to attack fully grown mountain goats.*

spiral flaring out and away from the head. The ram's horns are about $35\frac{1}{2}$ inches long and spread to 3 feet. The bighorn, on the other hand, have massive brown horns that curve up and back over the ears and then down and around past the cheeks in a C shape curl. Sometimes they are broken off near the tips, more often than not deliberately rubbed off against rocks when they threaten peripheral vision.

Dall sheep rams are 33 to 42 inches high at the shoulder and weigh up to 200 pounds; bighorn rams are 36 to 40 inches and weigh up to 316 pounds. The habits of the two are similar in that they live in areas seldom disturbed by humans. Both are excellent climbers.

Dall's sheep are found only at Denali National Park; the bighorn are seen at Badlands, Glacier, Rocky Mountain, Theodore Roosevelt, and Yellowstone. At Yellowstone in the summer, the bighorn has been seen on Mount Washburn in flocks of 40 to 50.

The three members of the North American cat family that inhabit national parks — mountain lion, lynx, bobcat — are abundant but so elusive that they are rarely seen. In fact the mountain lion, sometimes called the cougar, puma, or catamount, is so solitary and secretive that many rangers and naturalists have spent entire careers in the same area without ever seeing one.

At one time the mountain lion roamed throughout the North and South America. Today it lives mainly in the western United States, with some small populations in southern Florida. It weighs more than 200 pounds and measures 9 feet from nose to tip of tail. Its coat is generally yellowish to tawny above, white overlaid with buff below. Sightings in national parks are extremely rare, but there are two in which there are possibilities — Everglades and Zion.

The lynx and the bobcat are about the same size and smaller than the mountain lion. The lynx has a dense, soft, smoke-gray fur and large feet, giving the impression that it is much larger than its 20 pounds. It stands about 2 feet at the shoulder and, like the mountain lion, is solitary. Mostly nocturnal, it is seldom seen in national parks. The best chances for a sighting of a lynx are in Alaska, particularly at Denali and Katmai.

The bobcat too is secretive and solitary and is often taken for the lynx, although it has shorter legs and smaller paws. Found in a number of national parks — Acadia, Arches, Badlands, Glacier, Grand Canyon, Grand Teton, Great Smoky Mountains, Guadalupe, Joshua Tree, Kings Canyon, Lassen Volcanic, Mesa Verde, Mount Rainier, North Cascades Olympic, Petrified Forest, Redwood, Rocky Mountain, Sequoia, Shenandoah, Theodore Roosevelt, Voyageurs, Wind Cave, Yellowstone, Yosemite, Zion — opportunities are better for spotting in the Everglades.

INDEX

Page numbers set in **bold type** refer to illustrations

PICTURE CREDITS

Ardea 7, 11 bottom, 13, 14-15, 16, 17, 18, 20, 21 bottom, 23, 25, 29, 31 bottom, 34, 35, 38 top, 44 bottom, 49, 50-51, 51 inset, 53, 54-55, 56-57, 57, 60-61, 64-65, 69 top left, 69 top right, 69 middle, 70-71, 72-73, 74-75, 78 bottom, 79, endpapers **Click Chicago** Raymond G. Barnes 70 Leanard Lee Rue 71 **Bruce Coleman** 47, 67 **The Image Bank** Alex Stewart 10 **Frank Lane Picture Agency** half title, 4-5, 8-9, 19, 21 top, 22, 24, 26, 27, 30, 31 top left, 32, 32-33, 36-37, 38 bottom, 39, 40, 42, 44 top, 45 top, 52-53, 59, 62, 63, 64, 65, 66, 69 bottom, 72, 77, 78 top **National Parks Services** title page, 11 top, 31 top right, 41, 43, 45 bottom, 48, 77 inset
Front cover: **Ardea**
Back cover: **Bruce Coleman**

Multimedia Publications (UK) Limited have endeavored to observe the legal requirements with regard to the rights of the suppliers of photographic materials.